T

OLS

Forew

What began as a modest update to the Museum's galleries became a reworking of the entire building. The design focused on the enhancement of the visitor's experience, specifically the visitor's relationship to viewing art. We began by creating an entirely new entry sequence designed to prepare the visitor for the artistic treasures in the galleries.

An arcade enclosing a ramp within it slowly rises to the entry and parallels a reflecting pool. Together, these elements have a calming effect, removing the visitor from his or her hectic urban life. Modulated daylight, shade and shadow establish a cadence, beckoning the visitor forward.

In the short distance to the galleries, it is important that the visitor's eyes adjust to the lower light levels found there. The effects prepare and encourage the visitor to become immersed in the art.

Understated daylight became a theme used throughout the project, quietly guiding the visitor through the Museum's elemental forms—forms at once civic and welcoming.

– Rick Sundberg

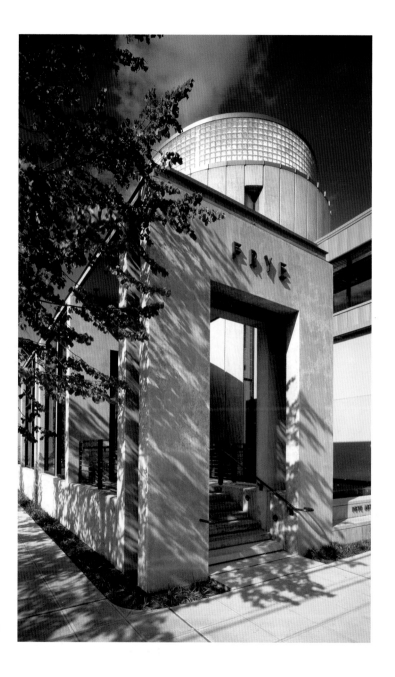

When I first walked into the rotunda that forms the entry of the Frye Art Museum, I was overcome with a sense of calm. Simultaneously austere and luxurious, the Frye is the kind of space that encourages you to slow down and savor all that's visible.

The transformation you experience begins at the covered entry walk—an abstract colonnade running parallel to a reflecting pool. The pool serves as a quiet organizing element, paradoxically providing the continuity and change that infuse the Museum. The pool mirrors the changing qualities of the Northwest sky. Together, the rotunda, arcade and reflecting pool provide the primary façade elements.

Standing in the rotunda, I looked up to an oculus set asymmetrically in a domed ceiling that appears to float within a glowing halo of light that falls subtly into the chamber. From the entry you can glimpse the galleries through oblique cuts in the circular room that slice from the projected center-point of the light oculus. Two paths originate from these cuts—one on a north-south axis and another on an east-west axis. These paths organize the primary gallery spaces as gentle light infuses them with a palpable glow.

The path along the north-south axis charts a course from the entry to the public spaces, passing through a series of small Special Exhibition Galleries that parallel the larger Permanent Collection Galleries.

The galleries are arranged in a clear and dignified plan, a parallel enfilade arrangement that terminates at the auditorium and café in the north end of the Museum. The galleries are generously proportioned, mindful of the art on exhibition. The reflecting pool, which runs alongside this path's exterior wall, is glimpsed through windows that sit tucked behind freestanding walls that exhibit art. The views and reflected sky brighten the galleries with an aura of dappled light. Daylight ushered in by light monitors washes down the Permanent Collection Galleries' walls and falls softly on the art below.

The public spaces comprise the café, auditorium and education wing. A Japanese veranda in the café overlooks the reflecting pool and offers a view of the rotunda. A courtyard, accessed from the café, lies next to the education spaces and provides a place of solace before or after a performance or lecture in the adjacent auditorium.

The second path, on the east-west axis, consists of the Special Exhibition Galleries. Small spaces lit by reflected light introduce each exhibit. The path then opens into a large gallery illuminated with the same natural glow as the Permanent Collection Galleries. Support spaces complete the east end of the building.

Olson Sundberg Kundig Allen has created a building that embodies rich simplicity by balancing rigorous logic and intuition. You see it in the plan. You feel it in the elegant details. But most important, you experience it in the gentle light that transcends the descriptive power of words. There is a term—liminal—that means "at the threshold between one state and another." The gentle light threaded throughout these spaces gives the Frye Art Museum a unique liminal quality—the quiet sense of transformation as light shifts color and place over the course of days and seasons. It is hard to capture, but easy to see.

BILLIE TSIEN
Tod Williams & Billie Tsien Architects

HISTORY

The Frye Art Museum, opened in 1952, was a gift to the people of Seattle from entrepreneur Charles Frye. It began as a collection of nineteenth-century German and Austrian paintings housed in a building designed by noted Northwest architect Paul Thiry. By 1994 the Museum had undergone a series of piecemeal renovations, and it was felt that a complete redesign was in order. This new design—including both a renovation and a substantial addition—merged the original Paul Thiry design with new architectural elements and brought the Museum up to current curatorial standards. Today, the Museum continues to showcase representational art and also exhibits contemporary art in diverse media. The Frye has been free to the public since its inception and attracts more than 100,000 visitors a year.

Charles Frye, at right, in an undated image

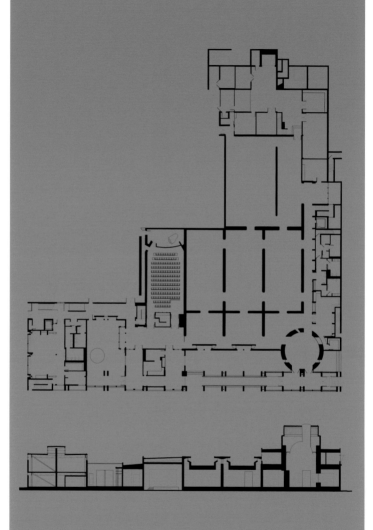

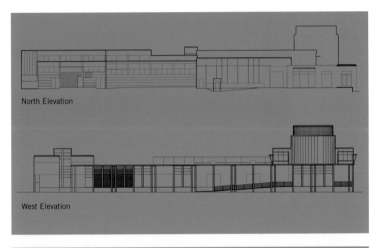

North Elevation

West Elevation

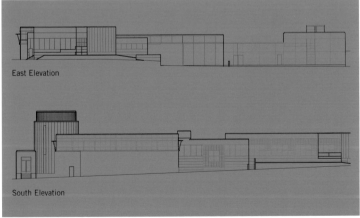

East Elevation

South Elevation

BELOW

The Museum is located in Seattle's First Hill neighborhood.

RIGHT (TOP TO BOTTOM)

Aerial views of construction progress. Top row: June 15, 1996; August 15, 1996.
Middle row: December 15, 1996; May 15, 1997. Bottom row: June 15, 1997;
September 15, 1997.

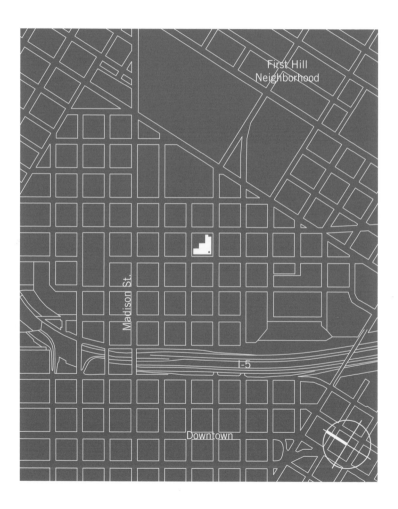

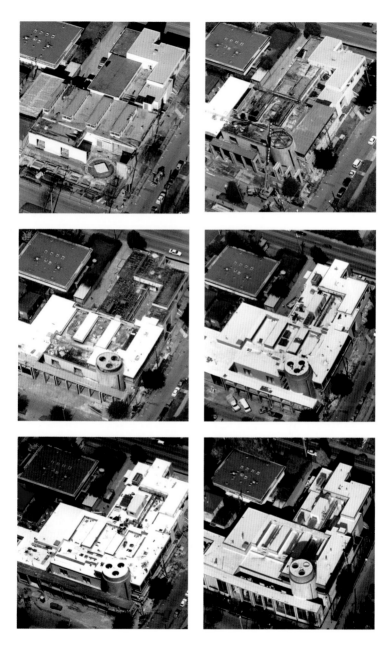

BELOW
Light levels are designed to diminish at five distinct intervals as the visitor moves from outside to inside through the entry sequence.

RIGHT
Points of light appear on the rotunda wall as the sun sets.

LEFT
Bronze doors signify the formal entry to the Museum. Bronze was selected for its
ability to record the patina of human use.

BELOW
The rotunda dome

PREVIOUS PAGE
Salon-style hanging is featured in this Permanent Collection Gallery.

LEFT / BELOW
Daylight slips around corners, reconnecting visitors with the outside to help eliminate fatigue.

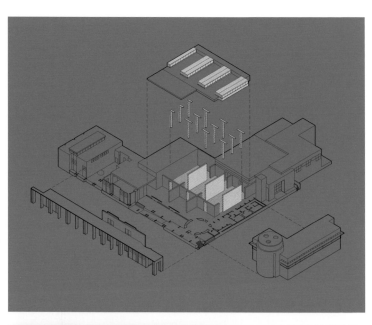

TOP LEFT

An exploded drawing shows major elements of the Museum pulled away to reveal the three Permanent Collection Galleries and their lighting strategy.

BOTTOM LEFT

During construction, the original light monitors were uncovered. Although they were not exposed in the original design, new technology made it possible to reveal them without sacrificing curatorial standards for the amount of daylight allowed to fall on a painting's surface.

BELOW

A computerized lighting model records the amount of daylight that falls on the paintings. This image was created by architecture students from the University of Idaho, Department of Architecture and Interior Design.

Illuminance [lc]
0   1.2   2.4   3.6   4.8   6   7.2   8.4   9.6   10.8   12

BELOW

Gallery benches are made of oak, steel and leather. The leather, like the bronze of the entry doors, will change as it acquires the patina of use.

RIGHT

Sketch for gallery benches

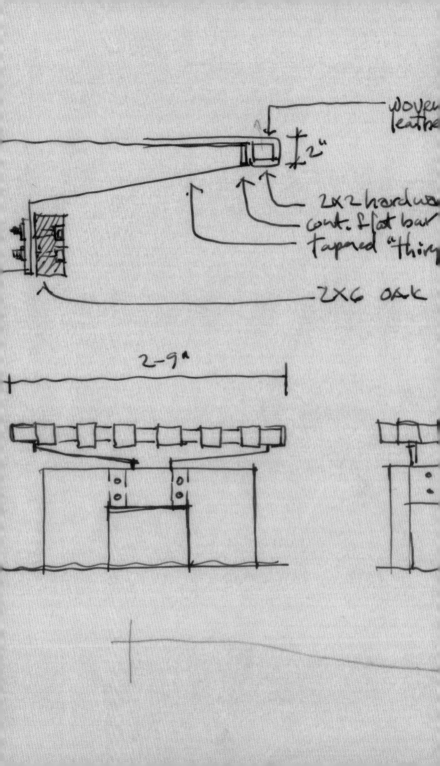

woven
leather

2"

2x2 hardwood
cont. flat bar
tapered "thin"

2X6 OAK

2-9"

MUSEUM DESIGN TEAM

Architect
Olson Sundberg Kundig Allen Architects
159 South Jackson Street, 6th Floor
Seattle, WA 98104
www.oskaarchitects.com

Design Team
Rick Sundberg, FAIA, Alan Maskin, Brett Baba, John Kennedy, Joshua Brevoort, Les Eerkes, Gladys Ly-Au Young, Kathryn Rogers Merlino

Structural Engineering
Monte Clark Engineering

Mechanical/Electrical Engineering
Affiliated Engineers, Inc.

Landscape Architect
Richard Haag Associates, Inc.

Civil Engineering
Rosewater Engineering

Gallery Lighting
Michael McCafferty

Building Lighting
Marietta Millett & Joel Loveland

Acoustical Engineering
Bruck Richards Chaudiere

General Contractor
Skanska USA Building Inc.

Awards
Plan-Section-Sentence Award – *Arcade* Magazine, 2000
Honor Award, AIA Northwest and Pacific Region Design Award, 1999
Honor Award, Architecture + Energy/Portland AIA Chapter, 1999

Special Thanks
Thanks to the Frye Art Museum for their cooperation in the preparation of this publication. Thanks also to Billie Tsien for her thoughtful words, and to the many artists whose legacy appears in the book, including contemporary artists Mark Ryden and Odd Nerdrum.